World Stage Press

ANASTASIA HELENA FENALD

Help Me, I'm Here

Poems to Myself

World Stage Press

World Stage Press

Help Me, I'm Here: Poems to Myself
© 2022, Anastasia Helena Fenald
ISBN: 978-1-952952-37-1

First Edition, 2022

Printed in the United States of America

Cover Design by Annie Cercone
Layout Design by Krystle May Statler

to the little girl who wanted to write poetry

CONTENTS

CONTENT WARNING:

This book contains descriptions about depression, anxiety, and suicidal thought which may be upsetting to some people.

FOREWORD

TO ME, SELF-LOVE WAS AKIN TO GRAFFITI: both could be acts of individual beautification, but to the uninitiated, their significance fades into obscurity. I used to think about self-love in this way. If Anastasia never asked me to edit this collection, I may have never given self-love anything more than a passing glance.

My opinion changed after reading through the first draft of Anastasia's *Help Me, I'm Here: Poems to Myself.* As I delved deeper into editing through her manuscript, I internalized how important this text is. Anastasia approached the theme of self-love in a striking fashion. I was captivated by the collaborative nature of her poems. Explicitly, her poems are in dialogue with one another. Implicitly, the use of first and second person pronouns blurs the identity of the narrator, lulling both Anastasia and the reader into the scene of the poem. Because it was a first draft, I talked to Ana about ways to control this ambiguity. It was then she revealed to me that many of these poems were taken from her middle school journal. I was floored by the love she had for her previous work's imperfection. I was floored because it awoke something in me I never realized before.

I began editing this collection when I was unhappy. I finished graduate school and ended up as a dishwasher with the night-owl shift. I remember jokingly confessing to Anastasia about how belittled the job-hunting experience left me. Unstated in all my self-deprecation was an implicit admission of how much I hated my past self for leading me to becoming my parents' worst investment. Thankfully, I know that isn't true; my parents have invested in landline phone alternatives since 2015. I'm also thankful that Ana's work has helped me realize something else about self-love.

I never told Ana this, but I always felt that this collection ended up being a haymaker to my ego. By including her childhood creations, she aims to go beyond ritualized self-deprecation: she aims to celebrate her growth and lineage. So, when her youngest narrator calls for help, the older narrators are there, not to condemn her, but to help her up. This is an element of self-love that I hadn't thought about but longed to incorporate into my own life. I offered to edit Anastasia's work as a favor, but I had a nagging suspicion that I would be the one indebted to her.

However, that thought runs contrary to the heart of this collection. Similar to the older narrators, I heard that Anastasia needed help editing. So, I was there. I imagine that Anastasia felt the same for me and my self-deprecation, and so her work straightened me out. I imagine that many readers read for a personal respite, so we are here for you. It is through this cooperation that everyone involved can begin to follow their life's continuity and grow from the experience. It is through this cooperation that I learned that self-love is admitting what you need and discovering that there will always be someone there to listen and encourage you to grow.

—Lincoln Der

Help Me, I'm Here

I'm Here

Poems to Myself

DEAR LITTLE ME

One day, you'll want to be called *Anastasia*. One day, you'll grow into me. One day, a little sooner than later, you learn you are the sum of your experiences, not your accomplishments.

One day, you'll understand why you feel lonely — that no love is greater than the love of yourself. What point is romance if you only possess a hollowed heart? What point is love if you're only swimming in self-hatred? One day, you'll stand next to your lonely and you will forgive her and welcome her in your open arms.

One day, you'll stop writing, too busy pursuing perfection than dreaming. This will be the hardest lesson to learn — you will never be perfect, your dreams aching the chance to grow. You sit here wanting to be perfect like a statue, like a work of art, but you are already glorious with your every breath.

One day that turns into many days, everything will hurt. Everything will be sand scraping against your skin, scarring you with the reminder of everything you could have been; everything will be suffocation as you stuff yourself small into countless boxes. Everything will be life static in your hands and you'll want to vanish, flicker away like Channel 3 when the TV turns off dead.

But one day, you'll write again; you'll see yourself in the mirror, pause at the ugly that reflects there and find beauty in the warm blood of your skin. One day, you'll wake up, ready to live, ready to be alive because you are tired of being cold, being empty, but still full of such doubt you've filled infinite Olympic swimming pools.

One day will become two days, then three days, then four days until all the above become every day. All the days meld together into love that shines like a constellation worth keeping, into light that survives years after we're gone. You will fall in love with yourself, leaving humility at the door, running fast into your heart.

You will succeed, chase dreams, and never stop; never letting life tell you're no one, you're nobody, when you are everything to me.

I know these are excruciating days; the pain sits so heavy on your shoulders. I know you want it all to end, but please wait for me. We are almost together, Little Me. You'll see — our kind of love? It's written in the stars.

Loving you now and forever,

Anastasia

HELP ME

(It's 2007. I'm 15.)

I have nothing left.
I know that now.
I tossed it all aside myself.
I wish I could just die.
I don't want this pain anymore.
I want it all to end.
I'm sick of it.
I can't do this.
I can't be me anymore.
My heart hurts.
It wants to stop beating.
Make it all stop.
… Is anyone listening?
Please?

I'M HERE

[15 years later.]

Can I — can I come near you?
Will you let me hold you?
Can I press your ear to my heart
so the steady beat becomes yours?

You are not alone, Little Me.
I'm here to love you.
I want to hear
every unsaid fear.

Is it okay if I take your hands
and stop them from tearing at yourself?
Please stop destroying this person who I adore.
You are not a burden to anyone.

Your kindness flows freshwater-sweet,
so eager to fill all the broken glass,
to parch the thirsty when we are desert dry.
Our heart is my favorite thing about us.

Would you believe me
if I said you will love living?
That the world is listening,
your story is just beginning.

In every dream, though,
I wish I could hold you,
just for a moment to say:
I'm here, I'm here

TIME TRAVEL

If I could go back in time,
I would tuck you in
every night;
play
barbies,
cowboys,
and make believe with you.
I'd watch our favorite movie
on countless loops
as we eat frozen TV dinners.

If I could go back in time,
I'd give you
all the hugs we wanted,
kiss your forehead
when we say
goodbye,
and love you
so loud
you'd wish
I'd be quiet.

If I could go back in time,
I'd listen to every secret
so you never feel alone
and be
the person
who never forgets to say,
"I love you."

If I could go back in time,
I'd be your
home.

STARS

(It's 2006. I'm 14.)

Are stars the eyes of all my loved ones who have died?
They seem to know that I look for the truth in them.
Stars guide me on the darkest nights,
torch the evil that remains in me.

Stars remind me of my family,
protect me from my fears like them,
guide my heart in all I do.
Stars know that my greatest friend is like them, too.

Take the truth and spell it out,
my friend, for you are my world.
Stars fade fast without me.
But you… stay with me like always.

Stars show me the other side of life,
my one and only loyal friend.
Stars fade without me again,
but I will wait for you.

MY TRUE NORTH

[16 years later.]

My blessed star, my oldest friend,
how you lit my darkest nights
and began again.
I am proof of all your wishes, Little Me.

Our past gleams like bright constellations.
I count the light years:
every secret, every memory —
all the days it takes to become me.

I hope I can be your guide
on the other side of time,
desperately longing
to keep you safe at night.

We are two comets
caught in each other's orbit,
time colliding my experience
with all your unknown.

I don't need to make a wish on us
as we soar through the skies.
You don't need to wait any longer,
for you're catching up to my stage in life.

JUXTAPOSITION

Time is our home;
a mirrored surface reflecting

the juxtaposition
of past and future.

All our seconds map
progress   forward.

THE SUN AND THE MOON

(It's 2003. I'm 11.)

Every morning the Sun rises
and greets me every day.
The warm sunshine on my face
makes me smile all day.
We laugh and we play
and warmth is all around me.
Time for the Sun to go
and a new face shall meet me.

At night, the Moon comes out to play.
I look at the starry sky
where the Moon plays hide-and-seek.
I feel the cool breeze playing with me and the Moon.
The moonlight shining down makes me feel like
an angel spreading my wings for the first time.
But now, the Moon sleeps
and a new day begins.

MUMMIFIED TIME

[19 years later.]

We stand
in the same spot
growing up,
watching dawn bloom over
the wrought-iron fence.
Sunrise drenches the desert
with pink and gold petals.
I still feel so small
when the sun heaves
itself over rooftops.

Later,
we walk
on cracked sidewalks,
desert weeds and breeze
our only company.
The moon hangs red, heavy,
and swallows the mountainous horizon;
consumes all the stars and satellites;
eats the flickering angry beacons
of cellphone towers;
and leaves us alone,
hungry in the dark.

There is no place like home
that reminds us
how little we've grown.
We still walk the dogs
up and down our hilly,
barren neighborhood
we did three dogs ago,
when the moon and sun
played make believe with us.

Yet, can we go back in time
to darkness under streetlights,
sing with celestial bodies,
and waltz with Santa Ana winds?
Can't we hear ghost barks
from dogs long past,
see empty land in the shadow
of the new housing developments of 2010?

Is it too late to still play?
I know the streetlights
mean "come home,"
but I want to stay
for a moment longer.
Your childish laughter
rings so sweet in my ear.

ATLASTASIA

We stand at night and day's fissure;
one hand holds our past,
the other holds our future.
We stand like Atlas, but we carry the light.
We don't know who has the worst burden.
Who is more tired?
It doesn't matter anymore.

In the ache of our shoulders,
call us the world.
In the spasm of our soul,
call us resilient.
In the dance of our life,
call us by our name:

Anastasia

MASTERPIECE OF THE SKY

(It's 2006. I'm 14.)

The sky is a blank canvas.
Sprites paint the dawn,
capture the falling moon and rising sun.
They bring clouds to life
with their brushstrokes back and forth.

At high noon, the sky is plain blue.
Clouds sway in the summer breeze.
The afternoon comes and the clouds submerge,
paints mixing the sunset purples and oranges.

When night falls, midnight blue with winking stars,
the sprites rest their brushes on storm clouds,
waiting for morning to come,
and paint the sky again.

HANG US IN THE GALLERY

[16 years later.]

My body is yours, Little Me.
Paint the sky you wish to see.
Our smile is moonlight,
our passion scintillating morning sun.

Atop our crown, we wear your beauty,
simple love and tender loyalty.
Small hands strap wings to our back,
joyous laughter sturdier than all the world's feathers.

Fly us higher, stain the sky with all your dreams —
my perfect little girl brimming with hope.
I exist because of you.
I exist because you wanted me to.

FRECKLES

Fireflies light the freckles
of your eyes
and in the darkness,
golden sun illuminates
the wonder of your spirit;
I tremble,
left breathless.

For you are my sun,
your soul my compass towards
something new
and I —
I fall to my knees
in reverent loyalty
as your smile contains
the Milky Way.

FINDING ME

(It's 2008. I'm 16.)

Here I am again,
lost on a path without light.
Only I can walk this journey,
this road of untouched darkness.

I sink my footsteps in the inky blackness.
Each step I make, more shadows try to stop me.
They want to stop me — me, from my road of Fate.
My quest, they want to ruin.

I trudge forward with every element against me.
It would be easier if I just gave up,
if I stopped moving, let the earth swallow me,
if I lost my sense of heart.

I could blend with the world.
Death would not harm me in death.
The void would be pure and harmless.
I could end all my suffering, my pain, my life.

But I will not.
I will walk my road in the darkness.
I will walk it alone.
I will find what is missing: I will find myself.

LOST AND FOUND

[14 years later.]

I want to say you find me easily,
but we know that isn't true.
Our journey is a lifetime long —
a labyrinth filled with apprehension.

Today you find me, though.
Your blistering hope incinerates
the phantoms that surround us,
fearless of who lurks in our shadows.

Tomorrow I'll think we're still lost,
our fire not bright enough
to read our maps and navigate
the forest of our thoughts.

But you're made from sturdy steel
as I am from chipped flint.
Together, we spark our own flames.
Together, our burns are ours to tame.

ROOM FOR HAPPINESS

You fear being alone —
afraid that the silence will wrap around you,
whispering your insecurities into your ear.

Sometimes you recoil at your reflection.
Beauty is only skin deep, the magazines say
but stretch marks score into your skin
and you buy plus-sized clothing.

You loathe being lonely —
afraid you are not worthy,
afraid you are no one's to love.
There is only one happiness in this life, to love and be loved,
a famous quote says.

Sometimes you pretend you are not broken;
that when you smile, it's true;
that when you close your eyes,
peace fills you.

In those moments,
you make room for happiness.

FINAL HOURS

(It's 2007. I'm 15.)

She began as a dim light,
but a light nonetheless.
She brightened every year,
and glowed with happiness.

I was the light,
long ago, it seems,
when I was loved and valued,
a time when I felt cherished.

I was only joy,
never wallowed in sorrow.
I opened my arms as a haven,
a lighthouse for all.

But time changed and so did people, too.
I sat there dimming,
my glow fading so slowly,
but no one seemed to notice.

They forgot me,
unwanted,
unneeded,
alone.

Here in my final hours,
my light dims.
The world passes on by a whim
and the spark inside me dies.

TO LIGHT A CANDLE

[15 years later.]

We drown
in a grave of our own.
All candle wax and wick,
melted to the nub.

There is still
some string left
to light
tonight.

I reach out &
grab the lighter,
flick the wheel
until there's fire.

It sucks
to be
alive
but,

death
is not
our
end.

We've
long
survived
our demise.

We've
long
survived
and live.

WORTHY

I am worthy of living.
I am worthy of existing.
I am worthy of being.
I am worthy.

AWAY

(It's 2006. I'm 14.)

The child cried all night.
Her self-esteem was very low.
She dreamed it away.

I'M WAITING

[16 years later.]

I wish I could
wipe your tears
on these nights
when you're little.

I wish I could
kiss your wounds
and make you
love yourself.

I wish I could
help you
right now.

I wish I could
heal you
right now.

I wish you knew
that I find you
in these brave poems
you write to no one.

My girl,
please don't cry.

I wish you'd hear me say:
"I love you,
I love you."

I'll be your dream,
I will come true.
For the day will come
when you'll love us, too.

WE ARE NOT ALONE

Help is admitting there's a problem;
a vulnerable confession;
a phone call away.

(please help me)

Help is a friend
or family.

(please someone help me)

Help is not being alone.
Help is my hand reaching out to you.

(please oh god help me)

[*shh, shh, I'm here, I'm here*]

I WANT TO RUN AWAY

(It's 2017. I'm 25.)

I want to run away.
I want to fade.
It's a lot easier than choosing
between the people I love most.
It's a lot easier than letting someone down.
Is it okay if I vanish?
Disappear into nothing?
I daydream of dying in a car crash.
I don't stop the oncoming traffic.
I slip into a crowd,
forcing myself to drown,
but the obligations
on my shoulders grip
my throat too tight.
I'm not meant for this world.
I'm not meant for love.
I'm not meant to be here.

THANK GOD YOU'RE STILL HERE

[5 years later.]

What if I told you
a year from then,
you let no one down?
That you forgive yourself
at age twenty-six?

That at twenty-seven,
you finally learn
there is no shame
in making errors?
Mistakes don't define
your character;
you're not broken?

What if I told you
there are answers
when you find a home
in our innocence?
When you rediscover comfort
in loving our Little Me
and write her poetry
she deserves?

What if I told you
I love you?
Is that enough to stay?

Please stay,
please don't run away.

I got you,
I got you.

DREAMING

I dream of a life
I want to live;
I am whole.

I dream in a world
made of daydreams;
their texture is the same as living.

I dream about
falling in love;
I fall in love with me.

I dream to dream
because life is too thin;
don't waste it just existing.

MOONLIT KISS

(It's 2007. I'm 15.)

Shimmer, shimmer, glorious moonlight.
Shine your moonbeams upon my lover's lips.
Gleam and gleam with the stars shining down.
Let me freeze this moment in time.

My love, so graceful and exquisite.
Her eyes sweet honey in your light.
She is so small compared to me.
I fear I will hurt her if I touch her.

She laughs and smiles while she looks at fireflies,
dances with the wind,
twirls so I can see her.
What else would I look at?

I walk in my trance to her.
Her smile only seems to widen.
I grab a hold of her and embrace her.
The air in my chest ceases to move.

Her small, fragile fingers grasp my shirt.
Her coffee hair brushes my hand.
The eyes that I love look upon me
and I upon them.

Time doesn't dare move.
Slowly, ever so tenderly,
I lower myself to her lips,
the moon reflected in her eyes.
Then we share a moonlit kiss.

MY FAVORITE KISS

[15 years later.]

I love us under gilded moonlight,
our precious declaration sewn into the stars,
our journey more than happenstance.

We are blessed eternal,
our past and present luscious love
that shines across our decades.

Our love is
laughter worth more than gold,
smiles more treasured than pearls.

I kiss our young heart.
the perfect combination of me and you:
the woman we'll one day be.

DAPPLED

/'dap(ə)ld/

adjective
marked with spots or rounded patches

the way that sun streams down
between tree branches
as you look up,
looking past the green,
the brown;
to seek blue and gold;
to signify
new beginnings
and hope.

sunshine kisses
look so good
on you.

I AM A FREE SPIRIT

(It's 2010. I'm 18.)

I am a free spirit —
Please do not reference "wild child."
I am a soul —
a being —
Far too unworldly
 to be claimed by others.
To this, I pose —
What emotions of others tie me down?
For nothing can chain me.
I may choose to wear weights of love
and adoration for what catches my fancy,
But please understand, my dear:
There is too much in my heart
to be isolated from unknowns.

WORLDLY TETHERS

[12 years later.]

We are not a free spirit now,
all our fears alphabetized.
Tried and true regrets for me and you;
never have I felt more youthful as I age.

Adult obligations
stamp out creative expression,
but we daydream anyway.
Another word for that is
"Resistance."

A contract signed on the dotted line
labeled "Growing Up" bears our signature.
So do our dreams,
printed for the world to read.

We are not a free spirit now;
too tangled in life,
in living,
yet adulthood is not our end.

We are children of the universe,
our time on Earth
not even as old
as sand.

Our time on Earth
a fragile blink,
but remarkable,
timeless chance.

AGING

Crow's feet at eyes
as we watch cartoons.

Going to bed early to prep
to be youngest supervisor in the room.

Laughing in pastels
as we eat too many cupcakes.

Reviewing reports
on employee performance.

Dancing to music
when no song plays.

Using overused cliches
with not a care in the world.

Choosing sparkling cider over wine
because it's more fun to drink.

Going home early
only to read all night in bed.

Growing up and
loving our inner kid.

DOUBT

(It's 2010. I'm 18.)

Doubt,
pure self-doubt,
plagues me.
Will I end up alone?
— where did all of you go?
Fear — of — being alone.
Strange, right.
Alone. Who is ever truly alone?
No one, I believe.

Doubt washes away into nothing.

(But why am I still lonely?)

HESITATIONS

[12 years later.]

Hesitation
is the root
of our
inadequacies.
Our heart
collapses
into a black hole,
sucks skin
off our muscle,
leaving all
our bones
exposed.

Perfection
does not preen—
a punch
cracks the mirror,
failures splinter
a thousand times.
Shards bite
our knuckles.

We are
not alone.
We are
our own
company.
An endless
circuit
of thoughts
and feelings
echoing
"I hate you,

I hate you—

—I hate me."

But

let's pretend
we are enough,
right now,
as we are,
an alright girl
with a stumbling
heart.

If only
we are
a brand-new star,
our light
bright enough
to slay monsters,
and people
bask
in our existence
because
we are
who
we are.

Hesitation
is the root
of our inadequacies
but I'm unsure
if I can be like this
for another decade.

You feel me?

RIPPED HURRICANES

A hurricane storms in my heart,
wanting something more
than what I am,
but for the first time,
I'm not terrified
to discover
who that is.

I want to rip this
negativity out of me,
not to destroy it,
but to greet my flaws
with my head held high.

BUTTERFLY

(It's 2006. I'm 14.)

Free to do anything.
Free to love anyone.
Free to be someone.
Free to be one with the skies.

Freedom to sing or listen.
Freedom to dance or stay still.
Freedom to smile or frown.
Freedom to fly the sky or walk the earth.

Freedom to love a gentleman.
Freedom to love an artist.
Freedom to love a poor man.
Freedom to love anyone.

Freedom to be a tycoon.
Freedom to be a warrior.
Freedom to be a lover.
Freedom to be a flyer.

Butterfly, don't you hear your freedoms?
Butterfly, you have so many chances.
Butterfly, you can be anyone and anything.
Butterfly, just fly.

METAMORPHOSIS

[16 years later.]

My butterfly girl,
freedom sings when we speak,
sparking fires beneath our armored wings.
We weld ourselves into our scales,
hammer out the denting dissonance we don't need.
We are limitless, a blueprint infinite,
our metamorphosis a continual process
never yielding to stagnate forces.

Butterfly,
Earth will try to suffocate us,
squash us, stomp us
with its rules and regulations.
But we know our own migration
entrenched in our DNA.
Our future is ours to take.
We are our only enemy —
our own demise
disguised as caution;
hesitation clips our wings.

No sky can encase us,
no gravity can anchor us.
There is freedom in our believing!
I believe it's faith worth keeping.

PASSING THOUGHT

Our place is amongst clouds;
our fingers skim
a trail in the blue sky.
Earth is a passing thought.

TO MY MOTHER

(It's 2006. I'm 14.)

As a rise at dawn
the dew shimmers on the petals,
the songbird sings a melody,
I can hear hymns from creatures.

In the garden, I wait for your return.
As in the middle of the night's rising moon
I wait to see you awake at dawn
or I shall wait forever.

As you awake, I know it is true
that you, my Mother, shall always return,
for upon the return that you make,
Mother, I shall greet by saying, "I love you!"

WE'RE ADULTS

[16 years later.]

The garden is ours now.
Mom's leaving it to us
to figure out.

The roses need tending,
the birds need feeding.
We forget to feed ourselves.

This is growing up.
The loneliness
that settles in
when we only
depend
on me,
on you,
on us.

I'm scared,
too,
Little Me.
Maybe the love
we cherish most
will be gone
in the morning.

We will
always be here,
little girl.
As we hold her hand,
the ghost of her palm
warm
between
our fingers.

DON'T EXIST

There's a universe where we don't exist.
And one where Mom can't have us.
In one, it's because of financial reasons.
In another, it's because she doesn't want us.

In one universe, she wants us so much,
but she miscarries in the third trimester.
Sometimes it isn't the right time.

In some universes,
she can't have children at all.
Or maybe she never had us —
she had another daughter instead.

There are universes where we commit suicide.
And sometimes, we wanted to change our mind too late.

Sometimes, sometimes,
sometimes.

There are universes where we die of old age,
and sometimes cancer,
and sometimes someone shot us
in the brain.

In those timelines and places,
in those universes,
we're dead right now.
But I'm not, at this moment.
In this universe,
I live like you,
I'm alive.

PETALS

(It's 2006. I'm 14.)

petals of roses
fall down to Earth's ground in cold
wait for spring to come

WE BLOOM

[16 years later.]

permafrost melting
puddles of fresh dew and wet dirt
our naked new beginning

PRUNING

I
take root in things
that rot under my feet.

Dig deep,
pluck my sins and virtues
and bury them inside me.

Wait
as darkness cuts days
shorter and shorter.

Become the sun
I never knew I needed
for my leaves.

I
stretch into the earth
and grow.

We weep
to nourish
all of me.

Bud
my sins
and good deeds.

I
do not bloom yet
but I will be beautiful.

I
take root
in new life and spring.

Take our fruit
and
stay with me.

WHEN DID I FORGET TO WRITE

(It's 2010. I'm 18.)

When did I forget to write?
Was it the inventions of friendships?
And true love? When did I forgo my talent?
To transcribe my words on paper
to fit into a society
that reorganized each one of us
into a place and a type,
forcing us to unwillingly belong?!

It is indescribable,
this adrenaline of writing,
wanting nothing more than
wanting to fulfill the want.
The words formed from my soul
as they used my fingers as their medium.
I have found my one & complete love.

WRITING DOESN'T DEFINE US

[12 years later.]

I sit here this year, aged thirty,
wanting the truth to be complicated
like the perceived miscommunication
that happens in every romantic comedy.

But like how romantic leads need honesty,
to talk to each other
instead of believing that Character A doesn't love
Character B because Character C told Character D
that Character A is going to marry Love Interest #2
to save the family farm...
We're not that complicated.

It's not that we forget to write, Little Me.
Just sometimes, Mom has cancer again,
or we're unemployed and miserable,
or we commute three hours a day
for a job that barely pays
but we do it anyway.

It's never that we forget to write —
we always want to write!
But sometimes we're tired.
Sometimes there's no time
between the 405 and 5 split.
Sometimes we actually don't want to.

And that's okay.

OUR MEANING

We're our own definition.
Our meaning shaped round:
top and bottom heavy,
a smile-disguised silhouette
keeps all our cunning.

Webster's doesn't know us,
our entry written over in new ink,
but I take my Times New Roman font
and live in the space between the spaces.

We are a striking bullet point nestled in paragraphs.

You can't look us up in the index,
but you'll stumble across us
in the anger that rests between
"helpful" and "helpless".

We thrive in our frustration;
flipping pages with a stinging paper cut,
our blood mixed with printed ink,
our legacy staining the dictionary.

We're our own definition,
the meaning changes every day.
Who we are tomorrow has no synonym.
Who we are today is original.
We define ourselves in our own language.

EXPLOSION

(It's 2007. I'm 15.)

One...
Two...
Three...
I will not be accountable for my actions.

Four...
Five...
Six...

RECYCLED DEBRIS

[15 years later.]

,

We own an angry heart,
soaked in gas,
housed by sugar glass
and we already lit the match.

We learned how to swallow ice.
Shove frostbite down our throats
to wear piercing sweet smiles
while we crumble that flame in our fist.

It is easier to gather up burns
in our palms like dinner mints,
maturity fragrant like bitter wine,
its taste unpleasant like holding our tongue.

How I long for no consequences:
to decimate our enemies with the dynamite
hidden by our new gentle disposition,
our words aching to be jagged as I am jaded.

VALID

Your anger is valid
as it simmers inside you.
Your bitter resentment
on your tongue – valid.
Your anxiety, your depression
as you submerge into the void:
valid and valid.
Your frustration is valid
as you cry irritated, *un*shameful tears.
Your envy? Valid, too,
as you wish you did more.
Your jealousy is just as valid
as you want what they have.

We do not need to ignore
the negativity in our lives.
It exists.
Let the feeling wash over you.
Accept it in the moment.
You are not *bad* because you feel bad.
Your worth is still priceless,
even when all you are is negative.
It's okay to have these moments.
It's okay to have emotions.

MY DREAM

(It's 2006. I'm 14.)

My dream.
Yes, the dream that I have.
The dream that I want to fulfill and claim my own.
The dream that will change the world...

Come, those who are broken.
Move step-by-step.
For I am here to catch you.
For this is my dream...

Never fear those who are alone.
March right up.
For I will join you.
For this is my dream...

Grab my hand
and tell me your story
of your broken life.
For this is my dream...

OUR DREAM

[16 years later.]

Our dream, you see,
manifests in cursive
as an elusive thing.

Ever changing,
unknown to you and to me,
only to be in moments of poetry.

Our dream, mine and yours,
has always been to —
(I don't know, and you don't know either.)

Let us tell a story instead
about how a woman went back in time
and found the girl she used to be.

Told her she loved her,
listened quietly about broken hearts
and even more so about broken feelings.

Our dream never made sense
in our timelines:
past and future.

But can't our dream, Little Me,
be us in motion as we scribble little notes
and tuck them away for later reading?

1 AM

1 AM and heart sings
words surge under skin;
have no pen and paper to write.

This is called *inspiration,*
a soul language
comfortable in a body bag;

air bursts through bones,
thoughts bleed from ears,
lyrics hum on tongue.

1 AM on desert shores,
poem waves lap at bed,
hands ache to catch word foam.

DOORWAYS

(It's 2008. I'm 16.)

I am at a standstill.
One door to my right.
One door to my left.
I can only choose one knob to turn.

The right door holds only problems.
I can fix this hurt, though.
I can be happy
if I give my boyfriend another chance.

The left door leads to a blank room.
I can paint fresh memories on the barren walls.
Become a new person.
I can be reborn.

I step closer to the left.
I am sick of sorrow, though.
I miss the way my smile feels.
I miss the taste of joy.

My fingers brush the bronze metal.
It chills my bones with pleasure.
The left door is so enticing.
I can be free.

But I don't want to be free yet.
He's just across the way.
I leave the blank door to nothingness.
I want to fix my heart.

CHANGE THE LOCKS

[14 years later.]

"Stop," I say
and grab your hand.
"Before you make your choice,
choose us instead.

I know you know us
because movie love is all we've wanted,
but what if I told you,
that it — that he won't be enough?

He's just a boy
who won't matter when we're old,
who'll never watch you grow
as I have."

I kiss your hand as a Queen to a Princess,
give you the chance to decide,
pray that this will feel right,
that with me, I'll leave our heart unbroken.

"Please trust me with your love,
my girl who loves so big,
my girl I'll always pick,
there's no one else so worth it."

ROMANTIC LOVE

Romantic love does not define you.
Romantic love does not define me.
Just because we only read
enemies to lovers,
oh, no!,
there was only one bed,
fake dating,
time travel,
excessive handholding,
monster boyfriends,
mutual pining,
surprise baby,
romance stories
every single day,
does not mean
we only exist
for
romance.

We just want a little love,
sans price tag.

SADLY

(It's 2010. I'm 18.)

Sadly, it is depression
that causes me to have inspiration.

Only in the hours, minutes, and days
when I feel so hopeless,
can I dare write something beautiful?

It is a curse, a cycle that must repeat itself,
because I truly do love writing,
but these are my true feelings.

School says that
the reader should never assume
that the poet is the speaker,
but aren't I the one speaking?

Aren't these my words?
Yet someone nameless gets the credit
for my ideas.

So, I embrace depression
like Edgar Allan Poe before me,
and, like him, we both use
the darkness of the heart
to feel worthy of paper and pen.

SADNESS STICKS TO US

[12 years later.]

I read your poems when I'm twenty-six.
A lifetime between our ever-changing being;
all the pain that weeps across time;
an immortalized diary on our hard drive.

Our sickness sticks to every document,
childhood cacophonous; anxiety cement mix
hardens in our breath,
and writing does not save us.

We drown from mafia feelings.
Sleep no longer with the fishes,
Depression's Hit Man rich once again
as we still scream ourselves hoarse,

and pretend nobody listens.

Sickness wants us to be alone,
isolates us to our cinder blocks in a noir film,
the ocean a new home that salts us,
our spirit preserved spread-eagle.

A lifeline dives deep
in Technicolor "Baywatch" glory,
performs CPR,
and signs us up for therapy.

MAINTAINING HAPPINESS

No one talks about
maintaining happiness.
It's always trying to be happy,
but never keeping it.

It's not normal — being happy.
I don't know what it means
when my life isn't in chaos.
I don't know what it means
not want to both love myself
but loathe myself.
A pendulum slices
the fraying edges
of my masked sanity.

I don't know what it means
to give to myself.
To fail without repercussion,
to trust myself, to be myself.
I don't know what it means
to stay happy,
but I want to try.
I want to know happiness.
I want to keep happiness.
I want to believe
in what I say to you,
Little Me.

I'll navigate my way
to happiness
with your love
as yarn string.

LOST IN MY HEART

(It's 2006. I'm 14.)

In all the places I've been,
all those maps I know,
all the streets I've memorized,
why do I get so lost in my heart?

There are so many twists and turns,
and no one is in sight;
it's only filled
with heartbreak and love.
I run and run and run,
never finding a place to go,
never finding anyone.
I just don't understand.
How am I lost in my heart?

LET'S ASK FOR DIRECTIONS

[16 years later.]

We have moons in our heart,
stars, too — ancient maps we can't read.
Our imagined reality blinded by
who we're told to be.

Shadows loom over a pulsing metropolis,
uncertainties and confidence are one-way streets;
intersections of expectations
never meet.

Traffic beats in steady desolation
with the engine's hum buzzing in our brain.
A useless distraction
as we slip away.

We listen to dangerous directions,
doubt guiding us down the wrong path,
but we don't speak up
and question.

Homeless love lingers on street corners.
A palm faces up towards us,
but we don't reach out, our hands tight
around the change in our pockets.

There are moons in our hearts,
full and round with dreams abound,
drowning in electric lights
that don't count.

"We are lost,"
we say to nobody, caught in our own eternity.
With you, Little Me, I want to know our possibilities;
count them like the stars we can't read.

Count them once, count them twice;
perhaps with time,
we can journey head over heels
to somewhere nice.

STABLE

/ˈstābəl/

adjective
(of an object or structure)
not likely to give way or overturn;
firmly fixed

our feelings as we keep them even;
we find balance by checking in with ourselves,
by asking what we need;
we ask for help and
directions to keep us steady
as we move throughout our days

another word for this is:
mindfulness

THE THOUGHT

(It's 2004. I'm 12.)

Every night I think of you,
I can barely speak.
I must look upon the stars to clear my mind.
For a moment, you are gone,
but then, you're back.
It's nice to think about you,
but it's hard
to get you out of my mind.
When I think of you, I feel happy,
yet I don't know what to call it;
calm, free to do anything,
free to say what it wants
like a secret you tell a friend.
You are an inspiration to me,
but so are all my friends.
I think about how everyone plays a role in my life.
The good times and the bad,
they have their part.
That thought too is true,
how you all play that role in my life.

GROWING UP TOO FAST

[18 years later.]

I can't get you out of my mind
that you wrote this poem about the boy you liked.
Days later, he groped your chest in broad daylight.

You fought back,
snarled like a Valkyrie and slapped him
into his weeklong suspension.

He's the first boy who puts his hands on you,
but he won't be the last.
You meet a dozen more who come at you.

They don't understand, they say.
Can't they enjoy what they see?
Aren't you wanting to feel sexy?

There's a long narrative in your life
where you don't get to say "no,"
their hands groping you without your consent.

You were taught as a child
that it was okay for grown men and growing boys
to lust for your body as if it was a prize.

Good thing you're a lucky one who could fight.
Good thing you were always in the right place.
Good thing you escaped every time.

REVOLUTION

We are a revolution of logic;
our own foundation of creation.
We build with hands that crack with hard work,
bleed with tenderness,
ache with effort.

We echo eras of womanly determination,
femme fatale and empowerment
smashing glass ceilings with words as damaging
as Molotov cocktails
to man-made brick buildings.

We are ourselves,
unlimited opportunity
dressed as personified ambition,
with credentials a mile high,
from home cooking
to open-heart surgery.

PERCEPTIONS AND NOTIONS

(It's 2013. I'm 21.)

Perceptions and notions
change in time,
but
the new definition of
self-reflection is
all-
ways
riddled with grief.

The you or it that used to be,
died — died — died so dead
it no longer breathed,
but you or it that used to be
is forever gone, yet stained you
with regrets and broken dreams.

MORNING PERIOD

[9 years later.]

I mourn for us
each time
we try to rearrange
our personality,
force ourselves
to be agreeable,
be normal,
be perfect.
It's nailing water
to a wall:
impossible.

Our own
expectations
crucify us.
Throbbing wounds
our only friend,
when we obsess,
when we stress
to our extinction —
nothing more than
the textbook definition
of insecure.

I cry, too,
at all the clarity
peeking through
in the moments
I catch our reflection
and find beauty in the heart.
We worry too much,
but I find wonder in your eyes,
hope dawning bright.

The scars
of your soul
cannot be ugly;
your existence
is a blessing,
your body
a holy place.

Would you believe me,
Little Me,
that you tinkered
with our heart unknowingly?
You forged it
with iron and gold,
made our heart
weather our darkest days.

This morning
we might hate ourselves,
and sometimes, that's still true.
But I know right here, right now,
there's no one I'd rather be
but you.

DIAMONDS

We are small.
Life oozes out of us,
our laughter carries
across the ocean
into their ear.

Our bones only stack so high.
In any room we enter,
we loom over everybody,
our personality
too much
for four walls.

We swallow them
and they stick
in the space
between our words
as we say:
"I love you."

We are breathtaking
because
we know
we are breathtaking.

We are a diamond now.
Every part of our soul's coal
now
shimmers
under the pressure.

They
can't take
that away.

BURN

(It's 2006. I'm 14.)

The grains of life's sand
burn all that seek hope and fun.
I hate the desert.

14 FREEWAY BEFORE FIRE SEASON

[16 years later.]

Blue moon thunderstorms
sing a siren song of rain.
Their kisses welt
the Mojave Desert green.
Bruising bushes pucker hilltops.
Orange poppies sunbathe naked.
Fast cars crawl molasses slow.
Obligations melt into
puddled forgetfulness
A distracted driver
enjoys Mother Nature,
sighs at her curves,
rounds the bend
of Soledad Canyon.
Rear-ends
the driver
dutifully paying
attention.
Everyone
is late
for work.

Today wears hot sun,
tomorrow a wildfire hums.
Poppies burn again.

FOREST FIRE STRONG

I was once a flickering candle,
my flame drowning in the wax.

At wits' end with my wick spent,
no more rope to make a life raft.

Burnout tasted the same as suffocation,
remnant smoke slipped between my fingers.

I was once a flickering candle
until I discovered paper.

I became firework explosions,
my sorrow fed with anger.

I engulfed the table and TV stand,
made the news by not staying silent.

I breathed oxygen as I ate the roof,
agency mine to choose.

I was my own bomb,
my shrapnel sharp and unafraid of where it rained.

I cauterized my own wounds,
scarred together into tight tissue.

I exploded years of expectations,
my flickering flame a forest fire strong.

I swallowed the bloated parts of me,
cleansed the rotten woods and backstreets.

In the ash I used to be from candle remains,
I plant roots in my new domain.

LOST CHILD

(It's 2006. I'm 14.)

Child lost and alone,
no warm hug for him in fear,
dies alone in dark.

BE MINE

[16 years later.]

Found child in my heart,
can I keep you, my darling?
Do you want to take my hand?

FIGURE EIGHTS

Paint soaks the pages
from our fingertips,
an expression of our love visible.
Bright blues and yellows
color the world.
Call us Picasso,
Call us van Gogh.
We transfer our soul
on thick paper.
We're infinity,
the alpha and omega,
our creations in motion.
We dip our hands in the paint again.
We dip our hands in life again.
We dip into ourselves again.
Have we always felt this good?

PERFECT HAPPINESS

(It's 2004. I'm 12.)

Her voice was calm.
She never raised her tone,
a smile of secrets plastered on her face.
Yet the girl still went on crying.

She watched the girl leave, feeling nothing.
The girl had destroyed her only means of happiness,
her only means of support.
But now that same girl cried, running away from her.

She needed her days before.
She was having a mental breakdown.
However, her friend, the girl, brushed her away
like she was nothing more than a bothering insect.

No one likes to be tossed aside with the garbage.
No one loves the emotion of being lonely.
No one wants to be forgotten, like they were nothing.
No one understands why friends are mean.

She gave up tears for courage.
She gave up her loneliness for friends.
She gave up her dependence on one for many.
She gave up her dull life for a brighter one.

When she saw her friend again and retold her tale,
her friend broke down in tears.
She felt nothing; there was no need to.
Girls just don't get mad, they get even.

MOVING ON

[18 years later.]

Our emotions still swell,
curl at high tide,
climb each notch of our spine,
only to snatch us in the undertow.

The serrated ocean floor forgives no one,
drags us through shipwrecks,
drowns us, keeps us,
as we forget how to swim.

No one is obligated to help us.
Our deep currents aren't easy to read,
because eighteen years later,
I can't remember who we were mad at.

FRIENDSHIPS UNFURL

Beautiful girl,
my darling, dear Pearl;
always
dreaming of sea swirls,
but friendships unfurl
sideways.
You sleep in sea curls.
I miss you, my girl,
today.

REPRESS

(It's 2012. I'm 20.)

Repress.
Repressing is what I do.
Down the drain — to the sewers of my heart,
where nothing can breathe.
Creatures of dark-ness fighting to
break free.
A box so tight that all
su-
ffo-
cates.
Can I still breathe if this pit is so deep?
No air in mybody&mind&soul.
I regress.
I repress.
All I feel is stress.
Stress stress stressstressstress.
And here, I lose the value of syntax and diction.
Oh, the underlying part of me — so deep.
So scary.
Do not escape.

YOU'RE NOT ALONE

[10 years later.]

We spend years
with tension boiling
the subcutaneous layers
between our
spirit and mind.

A lifetime where we
pinprick ourselves,
until nothing remains.

We spend years
stretched
to our
infinite end
because
no one
wanted
to tell us
something
broke
in our brain.

You spend
years in pain
because
no one
wanted to listen
about the chaos
swirling inside us
we couldn't name.

But I'm listening.
I know
your story.
I've memorized
it perfectly.

Take
my breath
and
breathe.
Take
my mind
and
body.
I'll be
gentle
with your
hallowed delicate heart.

Rest now,
my darling.
It's going to be okay,
close your eyes.
I'll fix everything.

A NOTICE FOR MY MENTAL ILLNESS

You stab the soft tissue of my trachea.
Claws scale the cliffside
where my larynx meets my esophagus,
and for a moment, I pretend you can't hurt me.

In your doomsday kit, you arson a fire,
choked smoke signals smog my breath.
My heart seizes as fear's flames
demolish the only exit.

I stutter stumbling sentences;
wobbly words weak;
reduced to repeating my regrets;
overwhelmed by the inferno of living.

You annex the slump of my shoulders.
My chest implodes under the pressure,
lighting up my whole body
in the wake of your burning bite.

I am so tired
as you tuck me in charcoal.
Exhausted embers
refuse to sleep.

Today, though, I scalpel you out of me.
I crush your windpipe,
watch you fight for breath as I fight for breath
because I'm sick of how sick you make me.

FADING ANGER

(It's 2006. I'm 14.)

A thunderstorm that finally clears.
Anger seems to disappear.
Rage built up inside like raindrops
in the morning time.

Emotion causing commotion
finally settles down.
I take my chances now while I can,
when I can be free.

Seeing the world for the first time,
hearing sounds I was deaf to,
smelling the aroma of nature,
feeling the ground like it's my last.

My anger blinded me.
I was too closed up inside like a shell.
I gave no one a chance to see me for real.
But I now know.

A thunderstorm that finally clears,
no more terrible clouds.
I feel the rays of sun
and wake up for once…

RENEW

[16 years later.]

There are days we become our own kindling,
forever scorching ourselves
until only dust remains.

Sometimes our fire is a lethal blade,
hostile and afraid.
It creates our backbone; it cuts us all the same.

Today we mix the mulch and till our fields.
Dew collects on the leaves.
Our pain a ghost under the simple blue sky.

The forecast calls for sunshine,
blessed kindness on my skin.
You never wanted to be without it.

Our resentment nourishes our acceptance,
our garden as green as we tend it —
little sprouts of change grow at our feet.

GLITTERING GROUND

I harvest
love that glitters the ground
with crisp sounds underfoot.

Confidence tastes ripe,
the promised juice tangy
with flesh soft for a stone fruit.

My passion paints the world
in solid seconds,
searing this into memory.

Insecurity's chill is absent;
yesterday's two-steps back forgotten,
tomorrow's forward steps on the horizon.

PUPPET MASTER

(It's 2006. I'm 14.)

They pulled my strings,
forcing me to dance.
Silly phrases sung
that do not belong to my lips

of wood and paint,
colors shrouding me with deception,
living lie after lie
of a marionette.

My Master enjoys in pain and sorrow,
forcing marionettes like me to live in pain and agony.
Yet we do not revolt against our Puppet Master,
for he pulls the strings, and we dance his web of lies again.

WE'RE ALMOST FREE

[16 years later.]

Anxiety finds home in our bones,
our joints heavy with emotional arthritis.
We forget what it's like to breathe
when our watch doesn't remind us.

We fall victim to our strings,
to fears that bind us, make us swing.
Like a corpse on Halloween,
except it's nothing like the movies.

We are monstrous, our own worst enemy:
our thoughts loop constantly,
our body frightened and frozen.
Our zombies crush us.

But our mouth still works,
shotgun-loaded and bullet-strong.
We are the heroine
of our own horror flick.

Anxiety strangles us
but my fingers can choke them, too.
"We aren't the sum of our failures,
for our flaws make us human!"

Don't call us a puppet,
we don't die this time.
We get out of the haunted house,
we get out alive.

QUIXOTIC

/kwik'sädik/

adjective
exceedingly idealistic; unrealistic and impractical

Society says that my dreams are *quixotic* –
unlikely,
unreal,
unimportant,
unneeded,
un-,
un-,
un-.
And I reply with a sledgehammer
smashing through barriers
and "no"s and
you're not good enough.
Wreck fucking glass houses
because, listen up,
asshole,
I got a bag full of dreams
heavy as stones.
I'm going to shatter everything,
break everything,
destroy everything
to get where I need to go.

WORDS PRESSED INTO MY FINGERPRINTS

(It's 2016. I'm 24.)

There are words pressed into my fingerprints,
waiting to be stamped out
for the world to see.

Stories etched into my palm lines,
my lifelines,
my reason for being.

These are hands that create
that ache with yearning,
to be better than yesterday.

They're sore from constant practice,
from erasing things inadequate,
to only begin again.

I have words in my fingerprints,
in my heart,
in me.

WE JUST LOVE TO WRITE

[6 years later.]

Our stories tower high,
brick-by-babbling brick
without a blueprint,
but somehow always written.

We speak one language:
intoxicating adoration.
Our creations possess our spare moments
as they write themselves into existence.

When day haunts our night,
anxious infatuation scores into our fingerprints,
every keystroke a golden 2 AM swan song —
the melody that brings our resurrection.

Oh, this is what it means
to sink into our soul, bathwater-warm.
Our one true north, our absolute belief
and it's all thanks to our most Littlest Me.

CHERRY PICKING

I pluck words off fruit trees,
steal sentences from teacups' steam,
borrow bad clichés from bird wings
and call them mine.

I crouch in soft syntax,
dig dirges for sad poetry —
live in the space between
rhythm and rhyme.

I am both mountaintop
and flooded forest,
floating in poems
walking on water.

COLOR

(It's 2006. I'm 14.)

drops of color flow
life is all but an artist
color keeps us alive

PUDDLE SPLASHING

[16 years later.]

Monotone gray rains
the past on horrid repeat,
but memories pool,
rainbows hope to our ankles,
leaving only a footstep.

TO MY FEET

I breathe,
every breath
pushes my emotions
down,
down,
down
until they rest
at my feet.

They travel along my frame,
seep into the small pores,
discolor my core.

It hurts,
like growing pains
when I was child
when my knees ached.
My dog Bella jumped on me
in the middle of the night
and I screamed.

I'm screaming still,
my emotions growing
like my skeleton
that holds me up throughout the day.

But sometimes
I pretend feelings don't exist,
bury them under
layers and layers
of "I'm fine."

SORRY

(It's 2004. I'm 12.)

I am sorry for what I do.
I can't restrain myself.
I don't understand why I do it.

Please give me another chance.
I know how cruel I can be,
but today I will be better.

The rude and hurtful things I say,
the jokes that just spill out,
please try to understand me.

I know we are different.
I know we are the same.
I just want to start over.

Please, I ask once again,
let's start over one more time.
I'm sorry for what I said.

I'M GOING TO DO BETTER

[18 years later.]

I'm sorry
for how
I've treated us
in all the years between;
knotted us
in self-loathing
and doubt,
wrecked our hearts
repeatedly.

We always
forgive,
but forgiveness
feels foreign
on our skin —
like fine silk
we can't afford
to cherish.

I'm sorry it takes
years for me
to heal.
I'm sorry
I drown you
in the cycle of
"Be good"
and
"You're not
good enough"
when you're
priceless to me.

I'm sorry
you'll write more
of these poems,
your mistakes
a badge
you think
you need
to wear.

Oh,
my darling,
my Little Me,
I want to swallow
all your apologies
because those words
are mine to keep.

I will build
a time machine
to take back
all I've done.
I will find you
in the Morse code
of every hurt
you never name.

CLEANSE

Come, let me wash the
day off your skin.
Forget the hardships as
I bathe you.
Let me love you in your
most vulnerable state.
There is nothing dirty about
your soul, nothing wrong
with your past.
You are perfect in this moment.
Clean because I see you —
all of you.
What supple skin my fingers kiss
and I only want to join you.

As I dry your skin,
keep you warm and protected,
please do not forget me.
Remember the gentle touch
of my soapy hands,
saying in all the silence
how I love you so.

NIGHTMARE

(It's 2006. I'm 14.)

You look into a mirror.
You see all your fears.
You try to run away, but you can't.
They find you wherever you are
to show you your worst fear.
They are a nightmare.
They are a feeling that will stay,
no matter what you do.
You will always be afraid to look into your heart.

You run and run forever.
You never stop.
They see you wherever you are.
You are a pawn in their game of death.
To them, you are nothing
but a game of life.
They rip your heart and mind out.
But they can never touch your soul.

DREAM EATER

[16 years later.]

We know nightmares.
How they become reality
as anxiety eats away at us.
We know suffocation, too,
our lungs burning in grad school,
failure cementing in our chest.

We call 911 on a fearful,
insomnia-fatigued morning.
"We're having a heart attack?"
we ask the operator.
But our impending sense
of doom is normal, they say.

We learn to rest with doom,
to move on with ourselves,
to focus on breathing.

Sometimes growing up
means we forget
what makes us anxious,
our demons buried
under a stack
of fresh memories.

Somehow,
our nightmares
flower into dreams.
Our hope
becomes
our currency
as we fall asleep.

We linger
on our blessings,
count them
like jumping sheep,
each one
a reminder
of good things.

We know
nightmares
sewed into our skin.
We know
how to live better,
hope
a dream come true,
constant friend.

PACIFIC DREAM

The sea —
Pacific dream,
float freely, water sings
lullabies with starry jewels
tonight.

Rest now;
wavey comfort
holds you tight; banishes
wicked shipwrecks from our evening
waters.

We sink
into her waves;
born again whence man came;
human skin our brave vessel when
awake.

I LACK—

(It's 2009. I'm 17.)

I
lack life —
experience.
Wisdom slips through —
my fingers.
Self-identity,
do I know it?
What sophistication of
living
have I mastered?
Accelerate,
advance
toward childhood?
Reverse to adulthood?
I lack —
enlightenment.
Give me sufferings.

WE LACK FORGIVENESS

[13 years later.]

We lack —
forgiveness.
No kind words
speak from our mouths.
Self-love,
what is that?
How can we love ourselves
when mistakes
are all we
make?
Move on
and grow
into a better person?
Is that possible
when
I'm stuck in the past?
I lack —
forgiveness.
But I'm giving myself
a second chance.

ENVY

We know envy,
like all the moles
we pretend are just beauty marks.

It sinks cracked, bitter teeth into us
and turns us slime green,
our spirit slippery, repugnant tar.

We are one monster movie away from monstrous,
when common sense smacks us
square in the heart.

Logic rushes in with the rose-tinted antidote
and shoves the vials down our throat.
It tastes like acceptance.

LOVE

(It's 2003. I'm 11.)

A boy and a girl and love at first sight.
What a beautiful thing to see.
The young lovebirds will see
what no one has ever seen before.
A kiss on the lips and a loved one to hold you at night
will bring an angel down to bless you with a family.
A child shall be born and young, sweet laughter
shall bring everyone closer.
Now the child is born and they are happily married.
They will be happy for the rest of their lives.
The love shall live on forever.
No one can take that away.
Their love is unbreakable no matter what you say.
So come and let them live forever.

BEING IN LOVE

[19 years later.]

Love is more simple
than wearing mom's wedding dress
and receiving the groom's kiss.

It's like laser tag
where you run and it's fun
to light up when you're hit.

Love is watching TV on a Friday night
where both of you fall asleep before nine
because life is quiet.

Love can't be defined by an image
when it's a symphony
of heartbeats and breaths.

It's leaping across a puddle
and they give you their hand
so you don't get your new shoes wet.

Love is where quick, harsh words
are followed by long discussions
and understanding.

It's…
happenstance and choice
rolled up in a paradox built for two.

Love is
your future,
bright and true.

ADULT LOVE

I can't write a love a poem,
for my love has no words.
Instead, it's about all the moments
I lay next to him and listen to his heartbeat.
It's the way I can fall asleep in his lap
after a long day at work.
In the afternoons, he rests his head
on my shoulder and cuddles close.

It's about all the places we've been
and the places we've yet to go,
in our friends we plan our lives around,
in our family we share.
In our family that will one day grow.

He said we are almost married,
that our vows of loyalty have already meant forever.
I have an invisible ring on my finger from him,
from all the promises and all the dreams.

I can't write a love poem,
but I can say that I love him;
our future gives me such hope
when I don't feel good enough.
When I feel lost and afraid,
his unshakable confidence reminds me
I am someone's partner in this world,
that to at least someone,
I am good enough.

PAINTED GIRL

(It's 2007. I'm 15.)

Lips painted crimson,
cheeks blushed cherry,
eyes of the darkest brown depths,
porcelain hands folded neatly upon her lap.

Short locks of russet,
a dress of pure blue,
upon a high shelf,
is where I watch the world.

I wait and wait upon my shelf,
seeing the world move by me.
Colors bright, colors true
dance in a fiery tango of chance.

Oh, how I long to join to them!
To move my lips of crimson!
To stand, to walk, to dance amongst them!
To remove myself from this shelf!

Yet here I am,
a painted girl,
who does not breathe a single breath of air!
I, me, shall forever remain here!

Lips painted crimson,
cheeks blushed cherry,
eyes of the darkest brown depths,
porcelain hands folded neatly upon her lap.

WEAR AND TEAR

[15 years later.]

The first time we speak,
we crack our lips and bleed.
All the words we've kept under lock & key
don't hurt to say; we're free.

Adrenaline kindles courage,
every hateful moment baptized as opportunity.
Our salvation echoes in our suffering,
all our fissures mapped our journey.

Who we are is more than skin-deep
when we tilt forward and smash who we've been.
When the dust settles after our destruction,
our personhood is still valid with our damage.

There is bravery in our existence.
The way we shout:
"I am broken, I am fractured,
I am good enough as is!"

We have authenticity
in our wrinkles, in our fine lines,
in the scars that pepper
our body and mind.

We are a shattered treasure,
prized trash has never looked better.
We keep our broken bits as one,
our wear and tear priceless vintage.

LONELY

No one tells us we will be lonely,
but we smile so big
so no one thinks we are lonely.
They call us a star, call us joy,
feel affection in our every breath,
but we are parched for affection.

No one tells us we will be lonely.
No one sees the longing
we have in our souls
to be noticed.
But we will be lonely,
always lonely,
always alone
in a room full of people.

No one tells us we will be lonely.
No one tells us that even if we love ourselves,
we have to make that declaration every day.
Boombox baring at the window of our heart,
stones tossed at the cracked glass,
but we are so tired.

The emptiness of loneliness
looks so comfortable
in these moments,
feels so comfortable
in these moments
of insecurity,
of self-doubt,
of fear
of never
being
good
enough.

But, dang, I wish
oh, how I wish
for someone
to
love
me.

Can anyone help me?

FORLORN SMILE

(It's 2007. I'm 15.)

I see her always.
My eyes drift towards that smile of hers.
She beams so brightly, so happily,
yet she dies inside.

Tears stream down her face.
Her heart breaks.
Her soul wanes.
Her spirit drowns.

Her voice muted,
her smiles so sad.
The glow that once lit her
dulls with time.

Still she smiles,
and smile she does.
Her heart beats unbearably,
yet she loves.

Her courage fades.
Her strength slips.
Her resolve breaks.
Her sense of self destroyed.

Yet she'll smile forever
and forever on,
for that's all she wishes for
till she passes on.

DON'T GOTTA SMILE

[15 years later.]

I remember that smile —
like clothespins pinching our cheeks,
revealing our braced and bucked teeth,
our delight black-lit with denial.

We pretended to walk on cloud nine;
didn't care that smoke and clouds looked the same;
didn't want to admit our pain;
just wanted to soak in sweet brine.

But I remember more
the nights we wept ourselves hoarse,
the days we crumbled under life's course,
yet kept wearing that pearly eyesore.

I'd do anything to erase that smile from memory
to set you free from all the people you tried to please;
tell you to frown and ignore their unease;
tell you there's no shame in being a cry-baby.

RESENTMENT

/rə'zentmənt/

noun
bitter indignation at having been treated unfairly

Irritated teakettle steaming screams;
blistered angered wounds
I strum to a guitar melody;
not the ideal woman kind of tune.

Too loud;
too quiet;
too fat;
too thin;
not enough;
too much;
not her;
but me;
told to be myself;
told don't be myself;
told to love myself.
No one gives instruction manual to do so.
Wrote my own instruction manual.
Unsure if it works;
gonna try anyway.

NEVER GIVE UP

(It's 2004. I'm 12.)

People say cruel things.
They will laugh at your work,
overlook the positivity of your whole heart.

But...

Never give up.
Never, ever.
Never give up in this world.

For life is sweeter when you try,
when you give yourself a chance,
when you hear the praise you deserve.

If you don't, you miss out on a chance in life.
You can ignore your one true love
and you won't ever be that sacrifice.

Never give up.
Never, ever.
Never give up in this world.

THANK YOU FOR BEING YOU

[18 years later.]

I stand with shaky knees,
immersed with uncertainty,
praying that my heart will stop stuttering.

Yet I find you, Little Me,
buried deep in memories —
a hopeful girl drenched in anxiety.

There are still days I can't love myself,
not in the way you'd dream,
but your demons are now mine to keep.

Your love is with me,
your song is my soul
serenading me through adulthood.

LEMON LOVE

Let me make you lemon honey tea, my little love.
No need to speak or tell me you're fine;
you don't have to lie to anyone tonight.

Let me take care of you and ease your cough.
I'll make you something soft to eat;
in sickness or in health, you're mine.

Rest your tired bones, be cozy by the fire;
I'll run my fingers through your hair
and I'll sing you a lullaby.

WIND BENEATH ME

(It's 2007. I'm 15.)

I don't remember when it happened.
When I started falling,
I lost all ties from my wings.
Thankfully the wind caught me,

screaming and yelling for you to grab my hand,
save me from the terror that lies in torment
where the death and decay and distortion reign
where I was afraid to go.

I lost sense of my reality, then terror struck.
And the nightmares that haunted me so,
the visions and premonitions that I hid from my eyes
tortured me until I paid attention.

Burning fire blazes of blue was I.
The skin ripped and shredded off my bones.
The tears would not fall because I had none left.
And I wondered, why did you not come for me?

In that pain, I finally remembered.
You tore my wings from me and let me fall.
You forced me away to the death and decay.
But the wind was always beneath me.

CRASH LANDING

[15 years later.]

We fell gasping,
burnt up our bones
and fragile ash.
A star crashed
into the earth
because of me.

I don't
remember
how long
we laid there
looking
for our spot
in the sky,
but it remained
dark.

We exhaled
the past —
our breath
new moisture
to nourish
a new girl:
our Future Me.

Covered in green
that buries us deep,
in new life
that eats the fruit
of our soil.
I'll crack our chest
and set you free.

You snap
our ribs
from our soul
with wobbly courage,
but blossom as yourself
to a time we can't follow.

We no longer fly,
but Mother Earth
looks good on you.
Run through her trees,
sow all your seeds.
Enjoy the future,
grow old without me.

HIDDEN LILACS

You hide under the lilacs,
your hair tangled in the stems of flowers
soaking up the starlight and sunshine.
Your mind the soil,
your heart the rain.

I join you under the lilacs,
lace our fingers together,
set down roots to ground me to now.
I relish in the soul you've given me,
I rest in the life I now have.

SUPERNOVA

(It's 2006. I'm 14.)

stars collapse
color of all shades shine
a new star is born

RESET

[16 years later.]

We're born
our starburst
unaccounted,
but stunning still.
Evolution spans
millions of years
& makes us
breathe,
makes us
stand on
two feet,
but somehow,
we yearn
for our beginning,
our necks
bent backwards,
eyes up
towards the sky
as our gaze
lingers on
the stars
at night.

LETTERED STARS

The stars
whisper
our name;
all our vowels
and
consonants
a perfect song
in gravity's mouth
as we
soar
through
galaxies
we don't know yet,
but want to.

WHAT I CAN'T GIVE YOU

(It's 2006. I'm 14.)

What I can't give you
is the one thing you wish
you had in your possession:
My pride.
You fools can't
accept what I have already to offer:
Myself.
You want me to die so
my rebirth can be a copy.
I refuse.
That is all I have to say.
Why can't I be me,
while you are able to be you?
Is it wrong for me to
have desires and opinions?
I am calling you all out,
each and every one of you,
who'd rather see me change
for your own benefit.
I will not
give up my freedom
of my personality for you.
Don't like me then hate me,
for I will hate you more.
I don't give a damn about you.
I'd rather be alone
than be surrounded by fake friends.
That's my choice.
All I can give you is me, but
you don't want me.
So hate me, but let me be me.

WHAT I CAN LEARN FROM YOU

[16 years later.]

How easily I've forgotten
that you are not always
the helpless damsel.
I turn the pages backward
and discover you've always
been our own knight.
You've slain dragons
with gleaming peer-pressurized scales,
uncaring if you're burnt to a crisp
because you wear weirdness
as a badge,
preening in their rage.
I need this now,
your unwavering strength
to help me weather all the gossip
that storms in my workplace.
Be my knight, Little Me.
Help me be the woman
who doesn't care about hierarchy.
Will you let me borrow
your backbone for a little while?
I'm gonna be me
just as you'll grow into being you
and we give no apologies.

CURRENCY

I read in a book
somewhere
that the best currency
in the world is attention,
but Fate did not look at me
and say *hey, you're gonna be one of the great ones.*

Obviously, Fate has not met the woman you've made of me.

YET I DO NOT MIND

(It's 2008. I'm 16.)

Ink stains my hands;
they are chapped and dry.
Colors dye my skin.
Yet I do not mind.

I do not mind
that you are childish,
that you are sweet and caring,
that you are you.

I do not mind
that you are silly,
that you make me oh so very angry,
that you hug me when I cry.

I do not mind
that you and I are very happy,
that we have ups and downs,
that you know me through and through.

I do not mind
writing poetry for you,
kissing you,
being with you.

I do not mind
being yours,
making you happy,
seeing you smile.

My hands are growing weak.
They hurt with every stroke they make.
They ache with new pain,
yet I do not mind.

I'LL LOVE YOU

[14 years later.]

We come
from a
patchwork family
where no one
gets good love
on the first try.

Every stitch
should not
be a sacrifice.
I know that now;
I wish
I'd known that then.

Our
tattered
edges
fray
along
the stories
where we
cherished
everyone
but us.

But in the warmth
by the fire,
grant me
your soft heart.
I'll quilt
our bruises
beautiful.

I know
nothing about
sewing,
yet
I do not
mind
every
needle prick
if it means
suturing
my love
for you.

PEACE

/pēs/

noun
freedom from disturbance; tranquility

no longer overthinking;
sight eyes believing;
meteor-shower wishes
covered by clouds on stormy nights;
diving into darkness
without needing a flashlight

curling up in clean sheets and warm pajamas;
the taste of mom's warm food in my belly after a rough day;
coming home to my puppy dog
after I've been away too long

SLUMBER LIKE LOVE

(It's 2006. I'm 14.)

In dreams, the soul awakes
like the sun at dawn.
It hears its other half
that rises with the twilight moon.

However, they shall never meet
except in the dreams of the mind.
Forever shall they ache in
slumber like love.

WE WAKE UP

[16 years later.]

The decades between us
feel like mere moments in memory:
twilight and sunrise our favorite hours
where time forgets
to begin again.

I can't remember
who stops dreaming first,
but our love wakes me up.
It's your soul I recognize in the mirror,
a twinkle in your eye like the best wishing star.

I don't know your embrace,
you don't know the strength of my palm,
but I close my eyes and your childish joy engulfs me.
No matter the time, no matter the place,
we are one and the same.

IF I DIE

If I die,
know I never suffered
from loving too much.

Break bread over my heart,
let the crumbs and the wine
nourish what I left broken.

When I die,
know that I love you so.
Take my soul and wear it
to keep you from the cold
on lonely nights.

In my goodbye,
please know I am waiting to say hello,
ready to take your hand
and welcome you home.

If I die,
when I die,
when I say goodbye,
know that my life with you
has never been more
perfect.

SING SWEETLY, O! KNIFE

(It's 2007. I'm 15.)

The twang of the knife carried terrifying weight,
the smooth, sharp tip allured me.
I needed pierce my heart.
It was… indescribable.
I wanted to slaughter myself.
The stars in the moonlit sky scrutinized me,
their beady eyes watched my every move,
telling me that they disapproved of what I was doing.
I didn't care.

The knife sang sweet music to me,
songs of the fragile line between life and death.
The world after me, the promise it held,
it was everything I wanted.
The wind tried to stop me.
Phantom hands grabbed my own,
slowly opening my fingers from the blade's grip
to steal the only thing that cared for me.
They didn't understand what I was doing.
They only saw good and evil.
But I was neither.
I was just tired of existing.
I dimmed, like dying stars.
My breath stopped as the wind blew less and less.
The moon could not reach me.

I was alone.
My heart raced in my chest.
I could perform what I pleased.
The knife sang so sweetly to me,
and my heart fluttered at his words.
I leveled the knife to be barely touching my inner wrist.
The metal was cold as ice.

My body shivered at the feeling,
and I cut my wrists.

Darkness washed over my bloody hands.
The moon that watched me kill dyed scarlet.
The soil below my bare feet turned sticky and metallic,
and I was the one who died.

NOT OUR END

(15 years later.)

I avoid this poem,
my heart suspends frozen;
I can't read this
without my skin crawling.

(this is why I waited until the end)

I can't read this
and be okay.

We were supposed
to die that day.

We had it planned,
we held the knife in our hand.
Death felt like our only friend.

If we died, if we said goodbye,
we wondered
who would notice?

I have no shame,
but only thanks.

We did not kill
ourselves at 15.
We gave life
another chance.

I carry this comfort
in my days now
when life is too much.
We don't give up.

We continue
to live.
We continue
to be.

We write this poetry,
a novel of a love letter,
in gratuitous currency
to forgive all our hate.

I forgive you, Anastasia.
I forgive who you used to be.
I forgive all the mistakes you made.
I forgive that you didn't want to live.

I love you, Little Me.
I love you so much.
I am so thankful you're here.
I am so thankful to be alive.

This book is not our ending
but our beginning to choosing
how we want
to live.

LITTLE ME

Thank you for living.
Thank you for always being.
Thank you,
thank you.

Love Always,
Anastasia

ACKNOWLEDGEMENTS

THIS POETRY COLLECTION has been an absolute labor of love. It has required having an open heart and mind and accepting the person I used to be. Without my younger self, this collection would not exist. Never once did she ever delete or burn her work. She kept it safe for the future because there was nothing more than she wanted then to be a poet. I'm proud to say that we've made it, Little Me. We're poets now! The world can read your poetry in its authenticity.

Help Me, I'm Here: Poems to Myself would also not exist without my dear friend, Lincoln Der. Not only has he written the foreword, but he also spent countless hours every week working with me to write this collection. His editing advice and creative writing understanding, along with his support, helped me chase my dream.

I would also like to thank Hiram Sims, Camari Carter-Hawkins, Kuahmel Allah and the Community Literature Initiative for creating a space for me to share and workshop my poetry. Los Angeles is a big city, but this organization has not only connected to me a diverse community of poets from all walks of life but has also welcomed me with open arms.

My poetry journey for the years 2020-2021 would not have happened without Oombi Flores. From the first day I heard them read their poem, I knew that I wanted to know them. Oombi has kept me accountable day after day, week after week, as we've worked on our manuscripts together. I would also like to thank the rest of my CLI Season 8 classmates such as James Coats, Karyn Renee, Tami Waters, Jerome Thomas, Lynda La Rose, Whitney Coble, Cristal Coleman, Aiyana Da'Briel, Miracle Morse, Ralonda Simmons, and Leanne Ingino.

I would also like to thank Annie Cercone for the beautiful cover design and Krystle May Statler for the layout designs. Without them, this book would not be as beautiful as it is!

This collection would also not exist without my best friend, Gigi Abdelhady. Never once did she doubt me, and she kept cheering me on when I felt at my lowest. Her constant love has kept me sane.

I'd also like to thank my partner, David Tran, who has embraced my love for writing and poetry. For buying me snacks so I can be fed while working or going to an event that's important for my inspiration, he's there. He has ingrained me confidence to be myself and to do what I want. I would literally not be as brave if it were not for him.

Lastly, but not least, this collection wouldn't exist without my mom, Dorothy McClelland and my babcha, Helen Napolitano. No matter what I wanted to do with my life, they have been there. They have spent all of my life supporting me and making sure I had whatever I wanted and needed. I love you both so much.

Thank you.

ABOUT THE AUTHOR

 Anastasia Helena Fenald (b. 1992) is a second-generation Ukrainian-Hispanic-American poet from Los Angeles and the Mojave Desert. She has a B.A. in Global Studies from the University of Riverside, California (2014) and an M.A. in Globalization and Development from the University of Sheffield, United Kingdom (2015). She spends most of her free time attending poetry workshops, performing at local open mics, and exploring Southern California.

Help Me, I'm Here: Poems to Myself is her debut poetry collection by the World Stage Press. She has also been published in Sheila-Na-Gig Online Journal, Acid Verse Literary Journal, The Sims Library of Poetry's Anthology Poems in Praise of Libraries, and innateDIVINITY books' anthology A Case for the Personhood of Trees and more.

Follow her on Instagram/Twitter: @anastasiafenald

Go to her website www.lospoetry.com for updates about poetry community events, updates about Anastasia Helena Fenald, and access to other authors in her poetry directory.

Follow Los Poetry on Instagram/Twitter: @lospoetry

HOTLINES

If you are experiencing a mental health crisis, or someone you love is in danger, the following resources can provide immediate help. You are not alone.

- **Suicide & Crisis Lifeline**: 988
- **Emergency**: 911
- **National Domestic Violence Hotline**: 1-800-799-7233
- **National Suicide Prevention Lifeline**: 1-800-273-TALK (8255); www.suicidepreventionlifeline.org
- **Suicide Prevention, Awareness, and Support**: www.suicide.org
- **Lifeline Crisis Chat**: https://www.contact-usa.org/chat.html
- **Crisis Text Line**: Text REASON to 741741 (free, confidential and 24/7). *Note, as of October 15, 2021, the free crisis counseling service is also available to Spanish-speaking texters.
- **Self-Harm Hotline**: 1-800-DONT CUT (1-800-366-8288)
- **Family Violence Helpline**: 1-800-996-6228
- **Planned Parenthood Hotline**: 1-800-230-PLAN (7526)
- **American Association of Poison Control Centers**: 1-800-222-1222
- **National Council on Alcoholism & Drug Dependency**: 1-800-622-2255
- **LGBTQ Hotline**: 1-888-843-4564
- **The Trevor Project**: 1-866-488-7386 or text "START" to 678678. Standard text messaging rates apply. Available 24/7/365. (Provides crisis intervention and suicide prevention services to lesbian, gay, bisexual, transgender, queer & questioning—LGBTQ—young people under 25.)
- **Veterans Crisis Line**: https://www.veteranscrisisline.net
- **International Suicide Prevention Directory**: http://suicideprevention.wikia.com/wiki/International_Suicide_Prevention_Directory

Made in the USA
Las Vegas, NV
31 July 2023

75478106R00100